ISBN 978-1-330-25824-8
PIBN 10004011

Similar Books Are Available from
www.forgottenbooks.com

KARMA

BY

ANNIE BESANT.

London:

Theosophical Publishing Society
7, Duke Street, Adelphi, W.C.

BENARES: THEOSOPHICAL PUBLISHING SOCIETY
MADRAS: *The Theosophist* OFFICE, ADYAR

1895

PRICE ONE SHILLING.

PREFACE.

Few words are needed in sending this little book out into the world. It is the fourth of a series of Manuals designed to meet the public demand for a simple exposition of Theosophical teachings. Some have complained that our literature is at once too abstruse, too technical, and too expensive for the ordinary reader, and it is our hope that the present series may succeed in supplying what is a very real want. Theosophy is not only for the learned; it is for all. Perhaps among those who in these little books catch their first glimpse of its teachings, there may be a few who will be led by them to penetrate more deeply into its philosophy, its science and its religion, facing its abstruser problems with the student's zeal and the neophyte's ardour. But these manuals are not written for the eager student, whom no initial difficulties can daunt; they are written for the busy men and women of the work-a-day world, and seek to make plain some of the great truths that render life easier to bear and death easier to face. Written by servants of the Masters who are the Elder Brothers of our race, they can have no other object than to serve our fellow-men.

KARMA.

Every thought of man upon being evolved passes into the inner world, and becomes an active entity by associating itself, coalescing we might term it, with an elemental —that is to say, with one of the semi-intelligent forces of the kingdoms. It survives as an active intelligence—a creature of the mind's begetting—for a longer or shorter period proportionate with the original intensity of the cerebral action which generated it. Thus, a good thought is perpetuated as an active, beneficent power, an evil one as a maleficent demon. And so man is continually peopling his current in space with a world of his own, crowded with the offspring of his fancies, desires, impulses and passions ; a current which re-acts upon any sensitive or nervous organisation which comes in contact with it, in proportion to its dynamic intensity. The Buddhist calls it his " Skandha ;" the Hindu gives it the name of " Karma." The Adept evolves these shapes consciously ; other men throw them off unconsciously. *

* The Occult World, pp. 89, 90. Fourth Edition.

No more graphic picture of the essential nature of Karma has ever been given than in these words, taken from one of the early letters of Master K. H. If these are clearly understood, with all their implications, the perplexities which surround the subject will for the most part disappear, and the main principle underlying karmic action will be grasped. They will therefore be taken as indicating the best line of study, and we shall begin by considering the creative powers of man. All we need as preface is a clear conception of the invariability of law, and of the great planes in Nature.

THE INVARIABILITY OF LAW.

That we live in a realm of law, that we are surrounded by laws that we cannot break, this is a truism. Yet when the fact is recognised in a real and vital way, and when it is seen to be a fact in the mental and moral world as much as in the physical, a certain sense of helplessness is apt to overpower us, as though we felt ourselves in the grip of some mighty Power, that, seizing us, whirls us away whither it will. The very reverse of this is in reality the case, for the mighty Power, when it is understood, will obediently carry us whither *we* will; all forces in Nature can be used in proportion as they are understood—"Nature is conquered by obedience"—and her resistless energies are at our bidding as soon as we, by knowledge, work with them and not against them. We can choose out of her boundless stores the forces that serve our purpose in momentum, in direction, and so on, and their very invariability becomes the guarantee of our success.

On the invariability of law depend the security of scientific experiment, and all power of planning a result and of predicting the future. On this the chemist rests, sure that Nature will ever respond in the same way, if he be precise in putting his questions. A variation in his results is taken by him as implying a change in his procedure, not a change in Nature. And so with all human action; the more it is based on knowledge, the more secure is it in its forecastings, for all "accident" is the result of ignorance, and is due to the working of laws whose presence was unknown or overlooked. In the mental and moral worlds, as much as in the physical, results can be foreseen, planned for, calculated on. Nature never betrays us; we are betrayed by our own blindness. In all worlds increasing knowledge means increasing power, and omniscience and omnipotence are one.

That law should be as invariable in the mental and moral worlds as in the physical is to be expected, since the universe is the emanation of the ONE, and what we call Law is but the expression of the Divine Nature. As there is one Life emanating all, so there is one Law sustaining all; the worlds rest on this rock of the Divine Nature as on a secure, immutable foundation.

THE PLANES OF NATURE.

To study the workings of Karma on the line suggested by the Master, we must gain a clear conception of the three lower planes, or regions, of the universe, and of the Principles* related to them. The names given to them indicate the state of the consciousness working on them. In this a diagram may help us, showing the planes with the Principles related to them, and the vehicles in which a conscious entity may visit them. In practical Occultism the student learns to visit these planes, and by his own investigations to transform theory into knowledge. The lowest vehicle, the Gross Body, serves the consciousness for its work on the physical plane, and in this the consciousness is limited within the capacities of the brain. The term Subtle Body covers a variety of astral bodies, respectively suitable to the varying conditions of the very complicated region indicated by the name psychic plane. On the devachanic plane there are two well-defined levels, the Form Level and the Formless Level; on the lower, consciousness uses an artificial body, the Mâyâvi Rûpa, but the term Mind Body seems suitable as indicating that the matter of which it is composed belongs to the plane of Manas. On the formless level the Causal Body must be used. Of the Buddhic plane it is needless to speak.

* See, for these, MANUAL I.

ÂTMÂ.

Plane		Principle	Vehicle	Body
Sushuptic		Buddhi	*Vehicle*	Spiritual Body
Devachanic		Manas	*Vehicles*	1. Mind-body 2. Causal Body
Psychic or Astral	Higher Psychic	Kâma-Manas	*Vehicle*	Subtle Body
	Lower Psychic	Kâma		
Phys ca		{ Linga-Sharîra { Sthûla-Sharîra	*Vehicle*	ɪ͡oss Body

Now the matter on these planes is not the same, and speaking generally, the matter of each plane is denser than that of the one above it. This is according to the analogy of Nature, for evolution in its downward course is from rare to dense, from subtle to gross. Further, vast hierarchies of beings inhabit these planes, ranging from the lofty Intelligences of the spiritual region to the lowest sub-conscious Elementals of the physical world. On every plane Spirit and Matter are conjoined in every particle—every particle having Matter as its body, Spirit as its life—and all independent aggregations of particles, all separated forms of every kind, of every type, are ensouled by these living beings, varying in their grade according to the grade of the form. No form exists which is not thus ensouled, but the informing entity may be the loftiest Intelligence, the lowest Elemental, or any of the countless hosts that range between. The entities with which we shall presently be concerned are chiefly those of the psychic plane, for these give to man his body of desire (Kâma Rûpa)—his body of sensation, as it is often called—are indeed built into its astral matrix and vivify his astral senses. They are, to use the technical name, the Form Elementals (Rûpa Devatâs) of the animal world, and are the agents of the changes which transmute vibrations into sensations.

The most salient characteristic of the kâmic Elementals is sensation, the power of not only answering to vibrations but of feeling them ; and the psychic plane is crowded with these entities, of varying degrees of consciousness, who receive impacts of every kind and combine them into sensations. Any being who possesses, then, a body into which these Elementals are built, is capable of feeling, and man feels through such a body. A man is not conscious in the particles of his body or even in its cells ; they have a consciousness of their own, and by this carry on the various processes of his vegetative life ; but the man whose body they form does not share their consciousness, does not consciously help or hinder them as they select, assimilate, secrete, build up, and could not at any moment so put his consciousness into rapport with the consciousness of a cell in his heart as to say exactly what it was doing. His consciousness functions normally on the psychic plane ; and even in the higher psychic regions, where mind is working, it is mind intermingled with Kâma, pure mind not functioning on this astral plane.

The astral plane is thronged with Elementals similar to those which enter into the desire-body of man, and which also form the simpler desire-body of the lower animal. By this department of his nature man comes into immediate relations with these Elementals, and by them he forms links with all the objects around him that are either attractive or repulsive to him. By his will, by his emotions, by his desires, he influences these countless beings, which sensitively respond to all the thrills of feeling that he sends out in every direction. His own desire-body acts as the apparatus, and just as it combines the vibrations that come from without into feelings, so does it dissociate the feelings that arise within into vibrations.

THE GENERATION OF THOUGHT-FORMS.

We are now in a position to more clearly understand the Master's words. The mind, working in its own region, in the subtle matter of the higher psychic plane, generates images, thought-forms. Imagination has very accurately been called the creative faculty of the mind, and it is so in a more literal sense than many may suppose who use the phrase. This image-making capacity is the characteristic power of the mind, and a word is only a clumsy attempt to partially represent a mental picture. An idea, a mental image, is a complicated thing, and needs perhaps a whole sentence to describe it accurately, so a salient incident in it is seized, and the word *naming* this incident imperfectly represents the whole; we say "triangle," and the word calls up in the hearer's mind a picture, which would need a long description if fully conveyed in words; we do our best thinking in symbols, and then laboriously and imperfectly summarise our symbols into words. In regions where mind speaks to mind there is perfect expression, far beyond anything words may convey; even in thought-transference of a limited kind it is not words that are sent, but ideas. A speaker puts into words such part of his mental pictures as he can, and these words call up in the hearer's mind pictures corresponding to those in the mind of the speaker; the mind deals with the pictures, the images, not with the words, and half the controversies and misunderstandings that arise come about because people attach different images to the same words, or use different words to represent the same images.

A thought-form, then, is a mental image, created —or moulded—by the mind out of the subtle matter of the higher psychic plane, in which, as above said, it works. This form, composed of the rapidly vibrating atoms of the matter of that region, sets up vibrations all around it; these vibrations will give rise to sensations of sound and colour in any entities adapted to translate them thus, and as the thought-form passes outward—or sinks downward, whichever expression may be preferred to express the transition—into the denser matter of the lower psychic regions, these vibrations thrill out as a singing-colour in every direction, and call to the thought-form whence they proceed the Elementals belonging to that colour.

All Elementals, like all things else in the universe, belong to one or other of the seven primary Rays, the seven primeval Sons of Light. The white light breaks forth from the Third Logos, the manifested Divine Mind, in the seven Rays, the " Seven Spirits that are before the Throne," and each of these Rays has its seven sub-rays, and so onwards in sequential subdivisions. Hence, amid the endless differentiations that make up a universe, there are Elementals belonging to the various subdivisions, and they are communicated with in a colour-language, grounded on the colour to which they belong. This is why the real knowledge of sounds and colours and numbers—number underlying both sound and colour— has ever been so carefully guarded, for the will speaks to the Elementals by these, and knowledge gives power to control.

Master K. H. speaks very plainly on this colour language ; He says ;

How could you make yourself understood, command in fact, those semi-intelligent Forces, whose means of communicating with us are not through spoken words, but through sounds and colours, in correlations between the vibrations of the two ? For sound, light and colour are the main factors in forming those grades of intelligences, these beings of whose very existence you have no conception, nor are you allowed to believe in them—Atheists and Christians, Materialists and Spiritualists, all bringing forward their respective arguments against such a belief—Science objecting stronger than either of these to such a degrading superstition.*

Students of the past may remember obscure allusions now and again made to a language of colours ; they may recall the fact that in ancient Egypt sacred manuscripts were written in colours, and that mistakes made in the copying were punished

* *Occult World,* p. 100.

with death. But I must not run down this fascinating by-way. We are only concerned with the fact that Elementals are addressed by colours, and that colour-words are as intelligible to them as spoken words are to men.

The hue of the singing-colour depends on the nature of the motive inspiring the generator of the thought-form. If the motive be pure, loving, beneficent in its character, the colour produced will summon to the thought-form an Elemental, which will take on the characteristics impressed on the form by the motive, and act along the line thus traced; this Elemental enters into the thought-form, playing to it the part of a Soul, and thus an independent entity is made in the astral world, an entity of a beneficent character. If the motive, on the other hand, be impure, revengeful, maleficent in its character, the colour produced will summon to the thought-form an Elemental which will equally take on the characteristics impressed on the form by the motive and act along the line thus traced; in this case also the Elemental enters into the thought-form, playing to it the part of a Soul, and thus making an independent entity in the astral world, an entity of a maleficent character. For example, an angry thought will cause a flash of red, the thought-form vibrating so as to produce red; that flash of red is a summons to the Elementals and they sweep in the direction of the summoner, and one of them enters into the thought-form, which gives it an independent activity of a destructive, disintegrating type. Men are continually talking in this colour-language quite unconsciously, and thus calling round them these swarms of Elementals, who take up their abodes in the various thought-forms provided; thus it is that a man peoples *his current in space with a world of his own, crowded with the offspring of his fancies, desires, impulses and passions.* Angels and demons of our own creating throng round us on every side, makers of weal and woe to others, bringers of weal and woe to ourselves—verily, a karmic host.

Clairvoyants can see flashes of colour, constantly changing, in the aura that surrounds every person each thought, each feeling, thus translating itself in the astral world, visible to the astral sight. Persons somewhat more developed than the ordinary clairvoyant can also see the thought-forms, and can see the effects produced by the flashes of colour among the hordes of Elementals.

ACTIVITY OF THOUGHT-FORMS.

The life-period of these ensouled thought-forms depends first on their initial intensity, on the energy bestowed upon them by their human progenitor; and secondly on the nutriment supplied to them after their generation, by the repetition of the thought either by him or by others. Their life may be continually re-inforced by this repetition, and a thought which is brooded over, which forms the subject of repeated meditation, acquires great stability of form on the psychic plane. So again thought-forms of a similar character are attracted to each other and mutually strengthen each other, making a form of great energy and intensity, active in this astral world.

Thought-forms are connected with their progenitor by what—for want of a better phrase—we must call a magnetic tie; they re-act upon him, producing an impression which leads to their reproduction, and in the case mentioned above, where a thought-form is re-inforced by repetition, a very definite habit of thought may be set up, a mould may be formed into which thought will readily flow—helpful if it be of a very lofty character, as a noble ideal, but for the most part cramping and a hindrance to mental growth.

We may pause for a moment on this formation of habit, as it shews in miniature, in a very helpful way, the working of Karma. Let us suppose we could take ready-made a mind, with no past activity behind it—an impossible thing, of course, but the supposition will bring out the special point needed. Such a mind might be imagined to work with perfect freedom and spontaneity, and to produce a thought-form; it proceeds to repeat this many times, until a habit of thought is made, a definite habit, so that the mind will unconsciously slip into that thought, its energies will flow into it without any consciously selective action of the will. Let us further suppose that the mind comes to disapprove this habit of thought, and finds it a clog on its progress; originally due to the spontaneous action of the mind, and facilitating the outpouring of mental energy by providing for it a ready-made channel, it has now become a limitation: but if it is to be gotten rid of, it can only be by the renewed spontaneous action of the mind, directed to the exhaustion and final destruction of this living fetter. Here we have a little ideal karmic cycle, rapidly run through; the free mind makes a habit, and is then obliged to work within that limitation; but it retains its freedom within the limitation and can work against it from within till it wears it out. Of course, we never find ourselves initially free, for we come into the world encumbered with these fetters of our own past making; but the process as regards each separate fetter runs the above round—the mind forges it, wears it, and while wearing it can file it through.

Thought-forms may also be directed by their progenitor towards particular persons, who may be helped or injured by them, according to the nature of the ensouling Elemental; it is no mere poetic fancy that good wishes, prayers, and loving thoughts are of value to those to whom they are sent; they form a protective host encircling the beloved, and ward off many an evil influence and danger.

Not only does a man generate and send forth his own thought-forms, but he also serves as a magnet to draw towards himself the thought-forms of others from the astral plane around him, of the classes to which his own ensouled thought-forms belong. He may thus attract to himself large reinforcements of energy from outside, and it lies within himself whether these forces that he draws into his own being from the external world shall be of a good or of an evil kind. If a man's thoughts are pure and noble, he will attract around him hosts of beneficent entities, and may sometimes wonder whence comes to him the power for achievement that seems—and truly seems—to be so much beyond his own. Similarly a man of foul and base thoughts attracts to himself hosts of maleficent entities, and by this added energy for evil commits crimes that astonish him in the retrospect. "Some devil must have tempted me," he will cry; and truly these demoniac forces, called to him by his own evil, add strength to it from without. The Elementals ensouling thought-forms, whether these be good or bad, link themselves to the Elementals in the man's desire-body and to those ensouling his own thought-forms, and thus work in him, though coming from without. But for this they must find entities of their own kind with which to link themselves, else can they exercise no power. And further, Elementals in an opposite kind of thought-form will repel them, and the good man will drive back by his very atmosphere, his aura, all that is foul and cruel. It surrounds him as a protective wall and keeps evil away from him.

There is another form of elemental activity, that brings about widespread results, and cannot therefore be excluded from this preliminary survey of the forces that go to make up Karma. Like those just dealt with, this is included in the statement that these thought-forms people the *current which re-acts upon any sensitive or nervous organisation which comes in contact with it, in proportion to its dynamic intensity.* To some extent it must affect almost everyone, though the more sensitive the organisation the greater the effect. Elementals have a tendency to be attracted towards others of a similar kind—aggregating together in classes, being, in a sense, gregarious on their own account—and when a man sends out a thought-form it not only keeps up a magnetic link with him, but is drawn towards other thought-forms of a similar type, and these congregating together on the astral plane form a good or evil force, as the case may be, embodied in a kind of collective entity. To these aggregations of similar thought-forms are due the characteristics, often strongly marked, of family, local and national opinion ; they form a kind of astral atmosphere through which everything is seen, and which colours that to which the gaze is directed, and they re-act on the desire-bodies of the persons included in the group concerned, setting up in them responsive vibrations. Such family, local or national karmic surroundings largely modify the individual's activity, and limit to a very great extent his power of expressing the capacities he may possess. Suppose an idea should be presented to him, he can only see it through this atmosphere that surrounds him, which must colour it and may seriously distort. Here, then, are karmic limitations of a far-reaching kind, that will need further consideration.

The influence of these congregated Elementals is not confined to that which they exercise over men through their desire-bodies. When this collective entity, as I have called it, is made up of thought-forms of a destructive type, the Elementals ensouling these act as a disruptive energy and they often work much havoc on the physical plane. A vortex of disintegrating energies, they are the fruitful sources of "accidents." of natural convulsions, of storms, cyclones, hurricanes, earthquakes, floods. These karmic results will also need some further consideration.

The Making of Karma in Principle.

Having thus realised the relation between man and the elemental kingdom, and the moulding energies of the mind—verily creative energies, in that they call into being these living forms that have been described—we are in a position to at least partially understand something of the generation and working out of Karma during a single life-period. A "life-period," I say, rather than a "life," because a life means too little if it be used in the ordinary sense of a single incarnation, and it means too much if it be used for the whole life, made up of many stages in the physical body, and of many stages without it. By life-period I mean a little cycle of human existence, with its physical, astral and devachanic experiences, including its return to the threshold of the physical—the four distinct stages through which the Soul passes, in order to complete its cycle. These stages are retrodden over and over again during the journey of the Eternal Pilgrim through our present humanity, and however much the experiences in each such period may vary, both as to quantity and quality, the period will include these four stages for the average human being, and none others.

It is important to realise that the residence outside the physical body is far more prolonged than the residence in it; and the workings of karmic law will be but poorly understood unless the activity of the Soul in the non-physical condition be studied. Let us recall the words of a Master, pointing out that the life out of the body is the real one.

The Vedântins, acknowledging two kinds of conscious existence, the terrestrial and the spiritual, point only to the latter as an undoubted actuality. As to the terrestrial life, owing to its changeability and shortness, it is nothing but an illusion of our senses. Our life in the spiritual spheres must be thought an actuality, because it is there that lives our endless, never-changing, immortal I, the Sûtrâtmâ, . . . This is why we call the posthumous *life the only reality, and the terrestrial one, including the personality itself, only imaginary.* *

During earth-life, the activity of the Soul is most directly manifested in the creation of the thought-forms already described. But in order to follow out with any approach to exactitude the workings of Karma, we must now analyse further the term "thought-form," and add some considerations necessarily omitted in the general conception first presented. The Soul, working as mind, creates a Mental Image, the primary "thought-form"†; let us take the term Mental Image to mean exclusively this immediate creation of the mind, and henceforth restrict this term to this initial stage of what is generally and broadly spoken of as a thought-form. This Mental Image remains attached to its creator, part of the content of his consciousness : it is a living, vibrating form of subtle matter, the Word *thought* but not yet *spoken*, conceived but not yet made flesh. Let the reader concentrate his mind for a few moments on this Mental Image, and obtain a distinct notion of it, isolated from all else, apart from all the results it is going to produce on other planes than its own. It forms, as just said, part of the content of the consciousness of its creator, part of his inalienable property ; it cannot be separated from him ; he carries it with him during

---

* *Lucifer*, October, 1892, art. " Life and Death."

† *Ante*, p. 12 *et seq.*

his earthly life, carries it with him through the gateway of death, carries it with him in the regions beyond death; and if, during his upward travelling through those regions, he himself passes into air too rarefied for it to endure, he leaves behind the denser matter built into it, carrying on the mental matrix, the essential form; on his return to the grosser region the matter of that plane is again built into the mental matrix, and the appropriate denser form is reproduced. This Mental Image may remain sleeping, as it were, for long periods, but it may be re-awakened and revivified; every fresh impulse—from its creator, from its progeny (dealt with below), from entities of the same type as its progeny—increases its life-energy, and modifies its form.

It evolves, as we shall see, according to definite laws, and the aggregation of these Mental Images makes the character; the outer mirrors the inner, and as cells aggregate into the tissues of the body and are often much modified in the process, so do these Mental Images aggregate into the characteristics of the mind, and often undergo much modification. The study of the working out of Karma will throw much light on these changes. Many materials may enter into the making of these Mental Images by the creative powers of the Soul; it may be stimulated into activity by Desire (Kâma), and may shape the Image according to the promptings of passion or of appetite; it may be Selfmotived to a noble Ideal, and mould the Image accordingly; it may be led by purely intellectual concepts, and form the Image thereafter. But lofty or base, intellectual or passional, serviceable or mischievous, divine or bestial, it is always in man a *Mental* Image, the product of the creative Soul, and on its existence individual Karma depends. Without this Mental Image there can be no individual Karma linking life-period to life-period; the mânasic quality must be present to afford the permanent element in which individual Karma can inhere. The non-presence of Manas in the mineral, vegetable, and animal kingdoms has as its corollary the non-generation of individual Karma, stretching through death to rebirth.

Let us now consider the primary thought-form in relation to the secondary thought-form, the thought-form pure and simple in relation to the ensouled thought-form, the Mental Image in relation to the Astro-mental Image, or the thought-form in the lower astral plane. How is this produced and what is it? To use the symbol employed above, it is produced by the Word thought becoming the Word outspoken; the Soul breathes out the thought, and the sound makes form in astral matter; as the Ideas in the Universal Mind become the manifested universe when they are outbreathed, so do these Mental Images in the human mind, when outbreathed, become the manifested universe of their creator. He peoples *his current in space with a world* *of his own.* The vibrations of the Mental Image set up similar vibrations in the denser astral matter, and these cause the secondary thought-form, what I have called the Astro-mental Image; the Mental Image itself remains, as has been already said, in the consciousness of its creator, but its vibrations passing outside that consciousness reproduce its form in the denser matter of the lower astral plane. This is the form that affords the casing for a portion of elemental energy, specialising it for the time that the form persists, since the mânasic element in the form gives a touch of individuality to that which ensouls it. [How marvellous and how illuminating are the correspondences in Nature!] This is the *active entity*, spoken of in the Master's description, and it is this Astro-mental Image that ranges over the astral plane, keeping up with its progenitor *, the magnetic tie spoken of, re-acting on its parent, the Mental Image, and acting also on others. The life-period of an Astro-mental Image may be long or short, according to circumstances, and its perishing does not affect the persistance of its parent; any fresh impulse given to the latter will cause it to generate afresh its astral counterpart, as each repetition of a word produces a new form.

The vibrations of the Mental Image do not only pass downwards to the lower astral plane, but they

---

* *Ante*, p. 13, and see also diagram, p. 9.

pass upwards also into the spiritual plane above it.* And as the vibrations cause a denser form on the lower plane, so do they generate a far subtler form —dare I call it form ? it is no form to us—on the higher, in the Âkâsha, the world-stuff emanated from the Logos Itself. The Âkâsha is the store-house of all forms, the treasure-house whereinto are poured—from the infinite wealth of the Universal Mind—the rich stores of all the Ideas that are to be bodied forth in a given Kosmos ; thereinto also enter the vibrations from the Kosmos—from all the thoughts of all Intelligences, from all the desires of all kâmic entities, from all the actions performed on every plane by all forms. All these make their respective impressions, the to us formless, but to lofty spiritual Intelligences the formed, images of all happenings, and these Âkâshic Images—as we will henceforth call them—abide for evermore, and are the true Karmic Records, the Book of the Lipikâ,† that may be read by any who possess the " opened eye of Dangma."‡ It is the reflection of these Âkâshic Images that may be thrown upon the screen of astral matter by the action of the trained atten-tion—as a picture may be thrown on a screen from a slide in a magic-lantern—so that a scene from the

---

* These words downwards and upwards are very misleading ; the planes of course interpenetrate each other.

† *Secret Doctrine,* i., 157-159.

‡ *Ibid.,* Stanza i. of the *Book of Dzyan,* and see p. 77.

past may be reproduced in all its living reality, correct ᵢₙ every detail of its far-off happening; for in the Âkâshic Records it exists, imprinted there once for all, and a fleeting living picture of any page of these Records can be made at pleasure, dramatised on the astral plane, and lived in by the trained Seer. If this imperfect description be followed by the reader, he will be able to form for himself some faint idea of Karma in its aspect as Cause. In the Âkâsha will be pictured the Mental Image created by a Soul, inseparable from it; then the Astromental Image produced by it, the active ensouled creature, ranging the astral plane and producing innumerable effects, all accurately pictured in connection with it, and, therefore, traceable to it and through it to its parent, each such thread—spun as it were out of its own substance by the Astro-mental Image, as a spider spins its web—being recognisable by its own shade of colour; and however many such threads may be woven into an effect, each thread is distinguishable and is traceable to its original forthgiver, the Soul that generated the Mental Image. Thus, for our clumsy earth-bound intelligences, in miserably inadequate language, we may figure forth the way in which individual responsibility is seen at a glance by the great Lords of Karma, the administrators of karmic Law; the full responsibility of the Soul for the Mental Image it creates, and the partial responsibility for its far-reaching effects, greater or less as each effect has other karmic

threads entering into its causation. Thus also may
we understand why motive plays a part so predomi-
nate in the working out of Karma, and why actions
are so relatively subordinate in their generative
energy; why Karma works out on each plane
according to its constituents, and yet links the
planes together by the continuity of its thread.

When the illuminating concepts of the Wisdom
Religion shed their flood of light over the world,
dispersing its obscurity and revealing the absolute
Justice which is working under all the apparent in-
congruities, inequalities and accidents of life, is it
any wonder that our hearts should go out in gratitude
unspeakable to the Great Ones—blessed be They !—
who hold up the Torch of Truth in the murky darkness, and free us from the tension that was straining
us to breaking-point, the helpless agony of witnessing
wrongs that seemed irremediable, the hopelessness of
Justice, the despair of Love :

Ye are not bound ! the Soul of Things is sweet,
  The Heart of Being is celestial rest ;
Stronger than woe is will : that which was Good
  Doth pass to Better—Best.

*   *

Such is the Law which moves to righteousness,
  Which none at last can turn aside or stay ;
The heart of it is Love, the end of it
  Is Peace and Consummation sweet.   Obey !

We may perhaps gain in clearness if we tabulate the threefold results of the activity of the Soul that go to the making up of Karma as Cause, regarded in principle rather than in detail. Thus we have during a life-period:

Plane.	Material.	Result.
Spiritual	Âkâsha	Âkâshic Images forming Karmic Record.
Psychic — Higher Astral		Mental Images, remaining in creator's consciousness.
Psychic — Lower Astral		Astro - mental Images, active entities on psychic plane.

The words "Man creates on" bracket all three planes.

The results of these will be tendencies, capacities, activities, opportunities, environment, etc., chiefly in future life-periods, worked out in accordance with definite laws.

THE MAKING OF KARMA IN DETAIL.

The Soul in Men, the Ego, the Maker of Karma, must be recognised by the student as a growing entity, a living individual, who increases in wisdom and in mental stature as he treads the path of his æonian evolution; and the fundamental identity of

the Higher and Lower Manas must be constantly
kept in mind. For convenience sake we distinguish
between them, but the difference is a difference of
functioning activity and not of nature; the Higher
Manas is Manas working on the spiritual plane, in
possession of its full consciousness of its own past ;
the Lower Manas is Manas working on the psychic
or astral plane, veiled in astral matter, vehicled in
Kâma, and with all its activities intermingled with
and coloured by the desire-nature; it is to a great
extent blinded by the astral matter that veils it, and
is in possession only of a portion of the total mânasic
consciousness, this portion consisting—for the vast
majority—of a limited selection from the more
striking experiences of the one incarnation then in
progress. For the practical purposes of life as seen
by most people, the Lower Manas is the " I," and is
what we term the Personal-Ego ; the voice of conscience, vaguely and confusedly regarded as super-
natural, as the voice of God, is for them the only
manifestation of the Higher Manas on the psychic
plane, and they quite rightly regard it as authorita-
tive, however mistaken they may be as to its nature.
But the student must realise that the Lower Manas
is one with the Higher, as the ray is one with its
sun ; the Sun-Manas shines ever in the heaven of
the spiritual plane, the Ray-Manas penetrates the
psychic plane; but if they be regarded as two, otherwise than for convenience in distinguishing their
functioning, hopeless confusion will arise.

The Ego then is a growing entity, an increasing
quantity. The ray sent down is like a hand plunged
into water to seize some object and then withdrawn,
holding the object in its grasp. The increase in the
Ego depends on the value of the objects gathered by
its outstretched hand, and the importance of all its
work when the ray is withdrawn is limited and con-
ditioned by the experiences gathered while that ray
has been functioning on the psychic plane. It is as
though a labourer went out into a field, toiling in
rain and in sunshine, in cold and in heat, returning
home at night ; but the labourer is also the proprietor,
and all the results of his labour fill his own granaries
and enrich his own store. Each Personal-Ego is the
immediately effective part of the continuing or
Individual-Ego, representing it in the lower world,
and necessarily more or less developed according to
the stage at which the Ego, as a totality or an
Individual, has arrived. If this be clearly understood
the sense of injustice to the Personal-Ego in its succession to its karmic inheritance—often felt as a
difficulty by the young student of Theosophy—will
disappear ; for it will be realised that the Ego that
makes the Karma reaps the Karma, the labourer that
sowed the seed gathers in the harvest, though the
clothes in which he worked as sower may have worn
out during the interval between the sowing and the
reaping; the Ego's astral garments have also fallen
to pieces between seed-time and harvest, and he reaps
in a new suit of clothes; but it is "he" who sowed

and who reaps, and if he sowed but little seed or seed badly chosen, it is he who will find but a poor harvest when as reaper he goeth forth.

In the early stages of the Ego's growth his progress will be extremely slow*, for he will be led hither and thither by desire, following attractions on the physical plane; the Mental Images he generates will be mostly of the passional class, and hence the Astro-mental Images will be violent and short-lived rather than strong and far-reaching. According as mânasic elements enter into the composition of the Mental Image will be the endurance of the Astro-mental. Steady, sustained thought will form clearly defined Mental Images, and correspondingly strong and enduring Astro-mental Images, and there will be a distinct purpose in the life, a clearly recognised Ideal to which the mind is constantly recurring and on which it continually dwells; this Mental Image will become a dominating influence in the mental life, and the energies of the Soul will be largely directed by it.

Let us now study the making of Karma by way of the Mental Image. During a man's life he forms an innumerable assemblage of Mental Images; some are strong, clear, continually reinforced by repeated mental impulses; others are weak, vague, just formed and then as it were forsaken by the mind; at death the Soul finds itself possessed of myriads

* See *Birth and Evolution of the Soul.*

of these Mental Images, and they vary in character as well as in strength and definiteness. Some are of spiritual aspirations, longings to be of service, gropings after knowledge, vows of self-dedication to the Higher Life ; some are purely intellectual, clear gems of thought, receptacles of the results of deep study ; some are emotional and passional, breathing love, compassion, tenderness, devotion, anger, ambition, pride, greed ; some are from bodily appetites, stimulated by uncurbed desire, and represent thoughts of gluttony, drunkenness, sensuality. Each Soul has its own consciousness, crowded with these Mental Images, the outcome of its mental life ; not one thought, however fleeting, but is there represented ; the Astro-mental Images may in many cases long have perished, may have had strength enough to endure but for a few hours, but the Mental Images remain among the possessions of the Soul, not one is lacking. All these Mental Images the Soul carries away with it, when it passes through death into the astral world.

The Kâma Loka, or Place of Desire, is divided into many strata as it were, and the Soul just after death is encumbered with its complete body of desire, or Kâma Rûpa, and all the Mental Images formed by Kâma-Manas that are of a gross and animal nature are powerful on the lowest levels of this astral world. A poorly developed Soul will dwell on these Images and act them out, thus preparing itself to repeat them again physically in its next life ;

a man who has dwelt on sensual thoughts and made
such Mental Images will not only be drawn to earth-
scenes connected with sensual gratifications, but will
constantly be repeating them as actions in his mind,
and so setting up in his nature stronger and stronger
impulses towards the future commission of similar
offences. So with other Mental Images formed
from materials supplied by the desire-nature, that
belong to other levels in Kâma Loka. As the Soul
rises from the lower levels to the higher, the Mental
Images built from the materials of the lower levels
lose these elements, thus becoming latent in consciousness, or what H. P. Blavatsky used to call
"privations of matter," capable of existing but out
of material manifestation. The kâma-rûpic vesture
is purified of its grosser elements as the Lower Ego
is drawn upwards, or inwards, towards the devachanic region, each cast-off "shell" disintegrating
in due course, until the last is doffed and the ray is
completely withdrawn, free from all astral encase-
ment. On the return of the Ego towards earth-life,
these latent images will be thrown outwards and
will attract to themselves the appropriate kâmic
materials, which make them capable of manifestation on the astral plane, and they will become the
appetites, passions and lower emotions of his desire-
body for his new incarnation.

We may remark in passing that some of the
Mental Images encircling the newly arrived Soul are
the source of much trouble during the earlier stages

of the post-mortem life ; superstitious beliefs presenting themselves as Mental Images torture the Soul with pictures of horrors that have no place in its real surroundings.* All the Mental Images formed from the passions and appetites are subjected to the process above described, to be remanifested by the Ego on its return to earth-life, and as the writer of the Astral Plane says :—

The LIPIKA, the great Karmic deities of the Kosmos, weigh the deeds of each personality when the final separation of its principles takes place in Kâma Loka, and give as it were the mould of the Linga Sharîra exactly suitable to its Karma for the man's next birth.†

Freed for the time from these lower elements, the Soul passes on into Devachan, where it spends a time proportionate to the wealth or poverty of its Mental Images pure enough to be carried into that region. Here it finds again every one of its loftier efforts, however brief it may have been, however fleeting, and here it works upon them, building out of these materials powers for its coming lives.

The devachanic life is one of assimilation ; the experiences collected on earth have to be worked into the texture of the Soul, and it is by these that the Ego grows ; its development depends on the number and variety of the Mental Images it has formed during its earth-life, and transmutes into their appro-

* See The Astral Plane, C. W. Leadbeater, pp. 24, 25.
† Ibid., p. 61.

priate and more permanent types. Gathering together all the Mental Images of a special class, it
extracts from them their essence: by meditation it
creates a mental organ, and pours into it as faculty
the essence it has extracted. For instance: a man
has formed many Mental Images out of aspirations
for knowledge and efforts to understand subtle and
lofty reasonings; he casts off his body, his mental
powers being of only average kind; in his Devachan
he works on all these Mental Images, and evolves
them into capacity, so that his Soul returns to earth
with a higher mental apparatus than it before
possessed, with much increased intellectual powers,
able to achieve tasks for which before it was utterly
inadequate. This is the transformation of the
Mental Images, by which as Mental Images they
cease to exist; if in later lives the Soul would seek
to see again these as they were, it must seek them
in the Karmic Records, where they remain for ever
as Âkâshic Images. By this transformation they
cease to be Mental Images created and worked on
by the Soul, and become powers of the Soul, part of
its very nature. If then a man desires to possess
higher mental faculties than he at present enjoys, he
can ensure their development by deliberately willing
to acquire them, persistently keeping their acquire-
ment in view, for desire and aspiration in one life
become faculty in another, and the will to perform
becomes the capacity to achieve. But it must be
remembered that the faculty thus builded is strictly

limited by the materials supplied to the architect;
there is no creation out of nothing, and if the Soul
on earth fail to exercise its powers by sowing the
seed of aspiration and desire, the Soul in Devachan
will have but scanty harvest.

Mental Images which have been constantly repeated, but are not of the aspiring character, of the
longing to achieve more than the feeble powers of the
Soul permit, become tendencies of thought, grooves into
which mental energy runs easily and readily. Hence
the importance of not letting the mind drift aimlessly
among insignificant objects, idly creating trivial
Mental Images, and letting them dwell in the mind.
These will persist and form channels for future out-
pourings of mental force, which will thus be led to
meander about on low levels, running into the
accustomed grooves, as the paths of least resistance.

The will or desire to perform a certain action, such
will or desire having been frustrated, not by want of
ability but by want of opportunity, or by circumstances forbidding accomplishment, will cause Mental
Images which—if the action be of a high and pure
nature—will be acted out in thought on the devachanic plane, and will be precipitated as actions on
returning to earth. If the Mental Image was formed
out of desire to do beneficent actions, it would give
rise to the mental performance of these actions in
Devachan ; and this performance, the reflection of
the Image itself, would leave it in the Ego as an
intensified Mental Image of an action, which would

be thrown out on to the physical plane as a physical act, the moment the touch of favourable opportunity precipitated this crystallisation of the thought into the act. The physical act is inevitable when the Mental Image has been realised as action on the devachanic plane. This same law applies to Mental Images formed out of baser desires, though these never pass into Devachan, but are subjected to the process before described, to be re-formed on the way back to earth. Repeated covetous desires, for instance, out of which Mental Images are formed, will crystallise out as acts of theft, when circumstances are propitious. The causative Karma is complete, and the physical act has become its inevitable effect, when it has reached the stage at which another repetition of the Mental Image means its passing into action. It must not be forgotten that repetition of an act tends to make the act automatic, and this law works on planes other than the physical ; if then an action be constantly repeated on the psychic plane it will become automatic, and when opportunity offers will automatically be imitated on the physical. How often it is said after a crime, " It was done before I thought," or " If I had thought for a moment I would never have done it." The speaker is quite right in his plea that he was not then moved by a deliberate thought-out idea, and he is naturally ignorant as to preceding thoughts, the train of causes that led up to the inevitable result. Thus a saturated solution will solidify if but one more crystal be dropped into it ; at the mere contact, the whole passes into the solid state. When the aggregation of Mental Images has reached saturation point, the addition of but one more solidifies them into an act. The act, again, is inevitable, for the freedom of choice has been exhausted in choosing over and over again to make the Mental Image, and the physical is constrained to obey the mental impulsion. The desire to do in one life reacts as compulsion to do in another, and it seems as though the desire worked as a demand upon Nature, to which she responds by affording the opportunity to perform.*

The Mental Images stored up by the memory as the experiences through which the Soul has passed during its earth-life, the exact record of the action upon it of the external world, must also be worked on by the Soul. By study of these, by meditation upon them, the Soul learns to see their inter-relations, their value as translations to it of the workings of the Universal Mind in manifested Nature; in a sentence, it extracts from them by patient thought upon them all the lessons they have to teach. Lessons of pleasure and pain, of pleasure breeding pain and pain breeding pleasure, teaching the presence of inviolable laws to which it must learn to conform itself. Lessons of success and failure, of achievement and disappointment, of fears proving groundless, of hopes failing realisation, of strength

* See the later section on the working out of Karma.

collapsing under trial, of fancied knowledge betraying itself as ignorance, of patient endurance wresting victory from apparent defeat, of recklessness changing into defeat apparent victory. Over all these things the Soul ponders, and by its own alchemy it changes all this mixture of experiences into the gold of wisdom, so that it may return to earth as a wiser Soul, bringing to bear on the events which meet it in the new life this result of the experiences of the old. Here again the Mental Images have been transmuted, and no longer exist as Mental Images. They can only be recovered in their old form from the Karmic Records.

It is from the Mental Images of experiences, and more especially from those which tell how suffering has been caused by ignorance of Law, that Conscience is born and is developed. The Soul during its successive earth-lives is constantly led by Desire to rush headlong after some attractive object ; in its pursuit it dashes itself against Law, and falls, bruised and bleeding. Many such experiences teach it that gratifications sought against Law are but wombs of pain, and when in some new earth-life the desire-body would fain carry the Soul into enjoyment which is evil, the memory of past experiences asserts itself as Conscience, and cries aloud its forbiddance, and reins in the hurrying horses of the senses that would plunge heedlessly after the objects of desire. At the present stage of evolution all but the most backward Souls have passed through sufficient experiences to

recognise the broad outlines of "right" and "wrong,"
i.e., of harmony with the Divine Nature and of
discord, and on these main questions of ethics a
wide and long experience enables the Soul to speak
clearly and definitely. But on many higher and
subtler questions, belonging to the present stage of
evolution and not to the stages that lie behind us,
experience is still so restricted and insufficient that
it has not yet been worked up into Conscience, and
the Soul may err in its decision, however well-
intentioned its effort to see clearly and to act rightly.
Here its *will to obey* sets it in line with the Divine
Nature on the higher planes, and its failure to see
how to obey on the lower plane will be remedied for
the future by the pain it feels as it blunders up
against the Law: the suffering will teach it what
before it knew not, and its sorrowful experiences will
be worked into Conscience, to preserve it from similar
pain in the future, to give it the joy of fuller knowledge of God in Nature, of self-conscious accord with
the Law of Life, of self-conscious co-operation in the
work of evolution.

Thus far we see as definite principles of karmic
Law, working with Mental Images as Causes, that:

Aspirations and Desires *become* Capacities.
Repeated Thoughts   ,,   Tendencies.
Wills to perform   ,,   Actions.
Experiences   ,,   Wisdom.
Painful Experiences   ,,   Conscience.

Karmic Law working with Astro-mental Images

seems better considered under the head of the working out of Karma, to which we will now turn.

THE WORKING OUT OF KARMA.

When the Soul has lived out its devachanic life, and has assimilated all that it can of the material gathered during its last period on earth, it begins to be drawn again towards earth by the links of Desire that bind it to material existence. The last stage of its life-period now lies before it, the stage during which it re-clothes itself for another experience of earthly life, the stage that is closed by the Gateway of Birth.

The Soul steps over the threshold of Devachan into what has been called the plane of Re-incarnation, bringing with it the results, small or great, of its devachanic work. If it be but a young Soul, it will have gained but little; progress in the early stages of Soul-Evolution is slow to an extent scarcely realised by most students, and during the babyhood of the Soul life-day succeeds life-day in wearying succession, each earth-life sowing but little seed, each Devachan ripening but little fruit. As faculties develop, growth quickens at an ever-increasing rate, and the Soul that enters Devachan with a large store of material comes out of it with a large increase of faculty, worked out under the general laws before stated. It issues from Devachan, clothed only in

that body of the Soul that endures and grows
throughout the Manvantara, surrounded by the aura
that belongs to it as an individual, more or less
glorious, many-hued, luminous, definite, and exten-
sive, according to the stage of evolution reached by
the Soul. It has been wrought in the heavenly fire,
and comes forth as King Soma.*

Passing on to the astral plane on its earthward
journey, it clothes itself anew in a Body of Desire,
the first result of the workings out of its past Karma.
The Mental Images formed during the past " from
materials supplied by the desire-nature, that had
become latent in consciousness, or what H. P.
Blavatsky used to call ' privations of matter,' capable of existing, but out of material manifestation,"
are now thrown outwards by the Soul, and immediately attract to themselves from the matter of the
astral plane the kâmic elements congenial to their
natures, and " become the appetites, passions, and
lower emotions of his [the Ego's] desire-body for
his new incarnation."† When this work is accomplished—a work sometimes very brief, sometimes
one that causes long delay—the Ego stands in the
karmic vesture he has prepared for himself, ready to
be "clothed upon," to receive from the hands of
the agents of the Great Lords of Karma the etheric

---

* A mystic name, full of meaning to the student, who understands
the part played by Soma in some ancient mysteries.

† *Ante*, p. 35.

double* built for him according to the elements he has himself provided, after which shall be shaped his physical body, the house which he must inhabit during his coming physical life. The individual and the personal Ego are thus immediately self-built, as it were—what he thought on, that he has become; his qualities, his "natural gifts," all these appertain to him as the direct results of his thinkings; the Man is in very truth self-created, responsible, in the fullest sense of the word, for all that he is.

But this man is to have a physical and etheric body that will largely condition the exercise of his faculties; he is to live in some environment, and according to this will be his outward circumstances; he is to tread a path marked out by the causes he has set going, other than those which appear as effects in his faculties; he has to meet events joyful and sorrowful, resulting from the forces he has generated. Something more than his individual and personal nature seems here to be needed; how is the field to be provided for its energies? How are the conditioning instruments and the re-acting circumstances to be found and adapted?

We approach a region whereof little may be fitly said, in that it is the region of mighty Spiritual Intelligences Whose nature is far beyond the scope of our very limited faculties, Whose existence may indeed be known and whose workings may be traced,

* Hitherto called the Linga Sharîra, a name that has given rise to much confusion.

but towards Whom we stand much in the position occupied by one of the least intelligent lower animals towards ourselves, in that it may know that we exist but can have no conception of the scope and workings of our consciousness. These Great Ones are spoken of as the Lipika and the Four Mahârâjahs. How little we can know of the Lipika may be seen from the following :

The Lipika, a description of whom is given in Commentary 6 of Stanza IV., are the Spirits of the Universe. . . . . [They] belong to the most Occult portion of cosmogenesis, which cannot be given here. Whether the Adepts—even the highest—know this angelic order in the completeness of its triple degrees, or only the lower one connected with the records of our world, is something which the writer is unprepared to say, and she would rather incline to the latter supposition. Of its highest grade one thing only is taught, the Lipika are connected with Karma—being its direct Recorders.*

They are the " Second Seven," and They keep the Astral Records, filled with the Âkâshic Images before spoken of†. They are connected

With the destiny of every man, and the birth of every child.‡

They give "the mould of the Linga Sharîra,"¶ which will serve as the type of the physical body suited for the expression of the mental and passional faculties evolved by the Ego that is to dwell therein, and

* *Secret Doctrine*, i., 153   † *Ante*, p. 27
‡ *Secret Doctrine*, i., 131.   ¶ *Ante*, p. 36.

They give it to " The Four "—to the Mahârâjahs, Who

Are the protectors of mankind and also the agents of Karma on Earth.*

Of these H. P. Blavatsky writes further, quoting the Fifth Stanza of the *Book of Dzyan* :

Four " Winged Wheels at each corner . . . for the Four Holy Ones and Their Armies (Hosts)." These are the " Four Mahârâjahs," or Great Kings of the Dhyân Chohans, the Devas, Who preside over each of the four cardinal points . . . These Beings are also connected with Karma as the latter needs physical and material agents to carry out its decrees.†

Receiving the mould—once more the " privation of matter "—from the Lipika, the Mahârâjahs choose for the composition of the etheric double the elements suited to the qualities that are to be expressed through it, and this etheric double thus becomes a fitting karmic instrument for the Ego, giving it alike the basis for expression of the faculties it has evolved, and the limitations imposed upon it by its own past failures and wasted opportunities. This mould is guided by the Mahârâjahs to the country, the race, the family, the social surroundings, which afford the most suitable field for the working out of the Karma allotted to the particular life-span in question, that which the Hindu calls the Prârabdha, or beginning, Karma ; *i.e.*, that which is to be worked out in the opening life-period. In no one life can the accumu-

* *Secret Doctrine,* i,, 151.   † *Secret Doctrine,* i., 147.

lated Karma of the past be worked out—no one instrument could be formed, no surroundings could be found, suitable for the expression of all the slowly evolved faculties of the Ego, nor affording all the circumstances necessary for reaping all the harvests sown in the past, for discharging all the obligations contracted towards other Egos with whom the incarnating Soul has come into contact in the course of its long evolution. So much then of the total Karma as can be arranged for in one life-period has a suitable etheric double provided for it, the mould of that double being guided to a suitable field. It is placed where the Ego may come into relations with some of such Egos, with whom it has been related in its past, as are present in, or are coming into, incarnation during its own life-period. A country is chosen where the religious, political and social conditions can be found which are suitable to some of its capacities, and afford the field for the occurrence of some of the effects it has generated. A race is selected—subject of course to the wider laws affecting incarnation in races, into which we cannot here enter—of which the characteristics resemble some of the faculties which are ripe for exercise, of which the type befits the incoming Soul. A family is found in which physical heredity has evolved the kind of physical materials which, built into the etheric double, will adapt themselves to its constitution ; a family of which the general or special physical organisation will afford play to the mental and passional natures

of the Ego. Out of the manifold qualities existing
in the Soul, and out of the manifold physical types
existing in the world, such can be selected as are
adapted to each other, a suitable casing can be built
for the waiting Ego, an instrument and a field in
which some of his Karma can be out-worked.
Fathomless to our short plummet lines as may be the
knowledge and the power required for such adaptations, we can yet dimly see that the adaptations can be
made, and that perfect Justice can be done ; the web
of a man's destiny may indeed be composed of threads
that to us are innumerable, and that may need to be
woven into a pattern of to us inconceivable com-
plexity : a thread may disappear—it has only passed
to the under side to come to the surface again
presently ; a thread may suddenly appear—it has
only re-emerged on the upper side after a long transit
underneath ; seeing but a fragment of the web, the
pattern may to our short sight be indistinguishable.
But as was written by the sage Iamblichus

What appears to us to be an accurate definition of justice
does not also appear to be so to the Gods. For we, looking
to that which is most brief, direct our attention to things
present, and to this momentary life, and the manner in which
it subsists. But the Powers that are superior to us know the
whole life of the soul, and all its former lives.*

This assurance that " perfect Justice rules the
world " finds support from the increasing knowledge

* *On the Mysteries*, iv., 4. See new edition of Thomas Taylor's
translation published by the T. P. S., pp. 209, 210.

of the evolving Soul; for as it advances and begins
to see on higher planes and to transmit its knowledge to the waking consciousness, we learn with
ever-growing certainty and therefore with ever-
increasing joy, that the Good Law is working with
undeviating accuracy, that its Agents apply it every-
where with unerring insight, with unfailing strength,
and that all is therefore very well with the world
and with its struggling Souls. Through the darkness rings out the cry, "All is well," from the
watchmen Souls, who carry the lamp of Divine
Wisdom through the murky ways of our human city.

Some of the principles of the working out of the
Law we can see, and a knowledge of these will help
us in the tracing out of causes, the understanding of
effects.

We have already seen that *Thoughts build Character;*
let us next realise that *Actions make Environment.*

Here we have to do with a general principle of
far-reaching effect, and it will be well to work it out
a little into detail. By his actions man affects his
neighbours on the physical plane; he spreads happiness around him, or he causes distress, increasing
or diminishing the sum of human welfare. This
increase or diminution of happiness may be due to
very different motives—good, bad or mixed. A
man may do an act that gives wide-spread enjoyment from sheer benevolence, from a longing to
give happiness to his fellow-creatures; let us say
that from such a motive he presents a park to a

town, for the free use of its inhabitants; another may do a similar act from mere ostentation, from desire to attract attention from those who can bestow social honours (say, he might give it as purchase-money for a title); a third may give a park from mixed motives, partly unselfish, partly selfish. The motives will severally affect these three men's characters in their future incarnations, for improvement, for degradation, for small results. But the effect of the action in causing happiness to large numbers of people does not depend on the motive of the giver; the people enjoy the park equally, no matter what may have prompted its gift, and this enjoyment, due to the action of the giver, establishes for him a karmic claim on Nature, a debt due to him that will be scrupulously paid. He will receive a physically comfortable or luxurious environment, as he has given wide-spread physical enjoyment, and his sacrifice of physical wealth will bring him his due reward, the karmic fruit of his action. This is his right; but the use he makes of his position, the happiness he derives from his wealth and his surroundings, will depend chiefly on his character, and here again the just reward accrues to him, *each* seed bearing its appropriate harvest.

Service rendered to the full measure of opportunity in one life will produce, as effect, enlarged opportunities of service in another; thus one who in a very limited sphere helped each who came in the way, would in a future life be born into a position where openings for giving effective help were many and far-reaching.

Again, wasted opportunities re-appear transmuted as limitations of the instrument, and as misfortunes in the environment. For instance, the brain of the etheric double will be built defectively, thus bringing about a defective physical brain; the Ego will plan, but will find itself lacking in executive ability, or will grasp an idea, but be unable to impress it distinctly on the brain. The wasted opportunities are transformed into frustrated longings, into desires which fail to find expression, into yearnings to help blocked by the absence of power to render it, whether from defective capacity or from lack of occasion.

This same principle is often at work in the cutting away from tender care of some well-loved child or idolised youth. If an Ego treats unkindly or neglects one to whom he owes affectionate duty and protection, or service of any kind, he will but too likely again find himself born in close relationship with the neglected one, and perhaps tenderly attached to him, only for early death to snatch him away from the encircling arms; the despised poor relation may re-appear as the much-honoured heir, the only son, and when the parents find their house left unto them desolate, they marvel at the "unequal ways of Providence" that deprive them of their only one, on whom all their hopes have been set, and

leave untouched the many children of their neighbour.
Yet are the ways of Karma equal, though past find-
ing out save for those whose eyes have been opened.

Congenital defects result from a defective etheric
double, and are life-long penalties for serious rebel-
lions against law, or for injuries inflicted upon others.
All such arise from the working of the Lords of
Karma, and are the physical manifestation of the
deformities necessitated by the errors of the Ego, by
his excesses and defects, in the mould of the etheric
double made by Them. So again from Their just
administration of the Law come the inwrought tendency to reproduce a family disease, the suitable
configuration of the etheric double, and the direction
of it to a family in which a given disease is heredi-
tary, and which affords the "continuous plasm"
suitable to the development of the appropriate germs.

The development of artistic faculties—to take
another type of qualities—will be answered by the
Lords of Karma by the provision of a mould for the
etheric double after which a delicate nervous system
can be physically built, and often by the guiding of
it to a family in whose members the special faculty
developed by the Ego has found expression, sometimes for many generations. For the expression of
such a faculty as that of music, for instance, a
peculiar physical body is needed, a delicacy of
physical ear and of physical touch, and to such
delicacy an appropriate physical heredity would be
most conducive.

The rendering of service to man collectively, as
by some noble book or speech, the spreading of ele-
vating ideas by pen or tongue, is again a claim upon
the Law, scrupulously discharged by its mighty
Agents. Such help given comes back as help bestowed on the giver, as mental and spiritual assis-
tance which is his by right.

We thus may grasp the broad principles of karmic
working, the respective parts played by the Lords
of Karma and by the Ego itself in the destiny of
the individual. The Ego supplies all the materials,
but the materials are used by the Lords or by the
Ego respectively according to their nature: the
latter builds up the character, gradually evolves
itself; the former build the mould that limits, choose
the environment, and generally adapt and adjust,
in order that the Good Law may find its unerring
expression despite the clashing wills of men.

FACING KARMIC RESULTS.

Sometimes people feel, on first recognising the
existence of Karma, that if all be the working out
of Law they are but helpless slaves of Destiny. Ere
considering how the Law may be utilised for the
control of Destiny, let us study for a few moments
a typical case, and see how Necessity and Freewill
—to use the accepted terms—are both at work and
at work in harmony.

A man comes into the world with certain inborn

mental faculties, let us say of an average type, with a passional nature that shows definite characteristics, some good, some bad; with an etheric double and physical body fairly well-formed and healthy, but of no specially splendid character. These are his limitations, clearly marked out for him, and he finds himself when he reaches manhood with this mental, passional, astral, physical "stock-in-hand," and he has to do the best he can with it. There are many mental heights that he is definitely unable to climb, mental conceptions which his powers do not permit him to grasp; there are temptations to which his passional nature yields, though he strives against them ; there are triumphs of physical strength and skill that he cannot achieve ; in fact, he finds that he can no more think as a genius thinks than he can be beautiful as an Apollo. He is within a limiting ring and cannot pass out of it, long as he may for liberty. Moreover, he cannot avoid troubles of many kinds ; they strike him, and he can only bear his pain; he cannot escape from it. Now these things are so. The man is limited by his past thoughts, by his wasted opportunities, by his mistaken choices, by his foolish yieldings ; he is bound by his forgotten desires, enchained by his errors of an earlier day. And yet *he* is not bound, the Real Man. He who made the past that imprisons his present can work within the prison house and create a future of liberty. Nay, let him *know* that he himself is free, and the fetters will crumble away from his limbs, and according to the measure of his knowledge will be the illusoriness of his bonds. But for the ordinary man to whom the knowledge will come as a spark, not as a flame, the first step towards freedom will be to accept his limitations as self-made and proceed to enlarge them. True, he cannot think as a genius thinks just yet, but he can think to the very best of his ability, and by-and-by he will become a genius; he can make power for the future, and he will. True, he cannot get rid of his passional follies in a moment, but he can fight against them, and when he has failed he can fight on, certain that presently he will conquer. True, he has astral and physical weaknesses and uglinesses, but as his thoughts grow strong and pure and beautiful, and his work beneficent, he is ensuring for himself more perfect forms in days to come. He is always himself, the free Soul, in the midst of his prison-house, and he can hew down the walls he himself builded. He has no gaoler save himself; he can will his freedom, and in willing it he will achieve.

A trouble meets him; he is bereaved of a friend, he commits a serious fault. Be it so; he sinned as thinker in the past, he suffers as actor in the present. But his friend is not lost; he will hold him fast by love and in the future he will find him again; meanwhile there are others round him to whom he can give the services he would have showered on his beloved, and he will not again neglect the duties that are his and so sow seed for similar loss in future

lives.   He has committed an open wrong and suffers
its penalty, but he thought it in the past else could
he not have wrought it now ; he will patiently endure the penalty he purchased by his thought, and
will so think to-day that his morrows shall be free
from shame.   Into what was darkness has come a
ray of light, and the light is singing to him :

> Ho ! ye who suffer ! know
> Ye suffer from yourselves.   None else compels.

The Law that seemed to be fetters has become
wings, and by it he can rise to regions of which
without it he could only dream.   ·

BUILDING THE FUTURE.

The crowds of Souls drift onwards along the
sluggish current of Time.   As the earth rolls, it
carries them with it ; as globe succeeds globe, they
too pass on.   But the Wisdom Religion is anew
proclaimed to the world that all who choose may
cease to drift, and may learn to outstrip the slow
evolution of the worlds.

The student, when he grasps something of the
meaning of the Law, of its absolute certainty, of
its unerring .exactitude, begins to take himself in
hand and actively to superintend his own evolution.
He scrutinises his own character, and then proceeds
to manipulate it, deliberately practising mental and
moral qualities, enlarging capacities, strengthening

weaknesses, supplying deficiencies, removing excrescences. Knowing that he becomes that on which he meditates, he deliberately and regularly meditates on a noble ideal, for he understands why the great Christian Initiate Paul bade his disciples "think on" the things that are true, honest, just, pure, lovely, and of good report. Daily he will meditate on his ideal; daily he will strive to live it; and he will do this persistently and calmly, "without haste, without rest," for he knows that he is building on a sure foundation, on the rock of the Eternal Law. He appeals to the Law; he takes refuge in the Law; for such a man failure exists not; there is no power in heaven or in earth that can bar his way. During earth-life he gathers his experiences, utilising all that comes in his way; during Devachan he assimilates them and plans out his future buildings.

Herein lies the value of a true theory of life, even while the theory rests on the testimony of others and not on individual knowledge. When a man accepts and partially understands the working of Karma, he can at once begin this building of character, setting each stone with deliberate care, knowing that he is building for Eternity. There is no longer hasty running up and pulling down, working on one plan to-day, on another to-morrow, on none at all the day after; but there is a drafting of a well thought-out scheme of character, as it were, and then the building according to the scheme, for the Soul becomes an architect as well as a builder, and wastes no more time in abortive beginnings. Hence the speed with which the later stages of evolution are accomplished, the striking, almost incredible advances, made by the strong Soul in its manhood.

MOULDING KARMA.

THE man who has set himself deliberately to build the future will realise, as his knowledge increases, that he can do more than mould his own character, thus making his future destiny. He begins to understand that he is at the centre of things in a very real sense, a living, active, self-determining Being, and that he can act upon circumstances as well as upon himself. He has long been accustoming himself to follow the great ethical laws, laid down for the guidance of humanity by the Divine Teachers Who have been born from age to age, and he now grasps the fact that these laws are based on fundamental principles in Nature, and that morality is science applied to conduct. He sees that in his daily life he can neutralise the ill results that would follow from some ill deed, by bringing to bear upon the same point a corresponding force for good. A man sends against him an evil thought; he might meet it with another of its own kind, and then the two thought-forms, running together like two drops of water, would be reinforced, strengthened, each by each; but this one against whom the evil thought is flying is a knower of Karma, and he meets the malignant form with the force of compassion and shatters it; the broken form can no longer be ensouled with elemental life; the life melts back to its own, the form disintegrates; its power for evil is thus destroyed by compassion, and "hatred ceases by love." Delusive forms of falsehood go forth into the astral world; the man of knowledge sends against them forms of truth; purity breaks up foulness and charity selfish greed. As knowledge increases, this action becomes direct and purposive, the thought is aimed with definite intent, winged with potent will. Thus evil Karma is checked in its very inception, and naught is left to make a Karmic tie between the one who shot a shaft of injury and the one who burned it up by pardon. The Divine Teachers who spake as men having authority on the duty of overcoming evil with good, based Their precepts on Their knowledge of the law; Their followers, who obey without fully seeing the scientific foundation of the precept, lessen the heavy Karma that would be generated if they answered hate with hate. But men of knowledge deliberately destroy the evil forms, understanding the facts on which the teaching of the Masters has ever been based, and sterilising the seed of evil, they prevent a future harvest of pain.

At a stage which is comparatively advanced in comparison with that of the slowly drifting, average humanity, a man will not only build his own character and work with deliberate intent on the thought-forms that come in his way, but he will begin to see the past and thus more accurately to guage the present, tracing Karmic causes onwards to their effects. He becomes able to modify the future by consciously setting forces to work, designed to interact with others already in motion. Knowledge enables him to utilise law with the same certainty with which scientists utilise it in every department of Nature.

Let us pause for a moment to consider the laws of motion. A body has been set in motion, and is moving along a definite line: if another force be brought to bear upon it, differing in direction from the one that gave it its initial impulse, the body will move along another line—a line compounded of the two impulses; no energy will be lost, but part of the force which gave the initial impulse will be used up in partially counteracting the new, and the resultant direction along which the body will move will be that neither of the first force nor of the second, but of the interplay of the two. A physicist can calculate exactly at what angle he must strike a moving body in order to cause it to move in a desired direction, and although the body itself may be beyond his immediate reach, he can send after it a force of calculated velocity to strike it at a definite angle, thus deflecting it from its previous course, and impelling it along a new line. In this there is no violation of law, no interference with law: only the utilisation of law by knowledge, the bending of natural forces to accomplish the purpose of the human will. If we apply this principle to the moulding of Karma, we shall readily see—apart from the fact that law is inviolable—that there is no "interference with Karma," when we modify its action by knowledge. We are using Karmic force to affect Karmic results, and once more we conquer Nature by obedience.

Let us now suppose that the advanced student, glancing backwards over the past, sees lines of past Karma converging to a point of action of an undesirable kind ; he can introduce a new force among these converging energies, and so modify the event, which must be the resultant of *all* the forces concerned in its generation and ripening. For such action he requires knowledge, not only the power to see the past and to trace the lines which connect it with the present, but also to calculate exactly the influence that the force he introduces will exercise as modifying the resultant, and further the effects that will flow from this resultant considered as cause. In this way he may lessen or destroy the results of evil wrought by himself in the past, by the good forces he pours forth into his Karmic stream ; he cannot undo the past, he cannot destroy it, but so far as its effects are still in the future he can modify them or reverse them, by the new forces he brings to bear as causes taking part in their production. In all this he is merely utilising the law, and he works with the certainty of the scientist, who balances one force against another and, unable to destroy a unit of energy, can yet make a body move as he will by a calculation of angles and of moments. Similarly Karma may be accelerated or delayed, and thus again will undergo modification by the action of the surroundings amid which it is worked out.

Let us put the same thing again a little differently, for the conception is an important and a fruitful one. As knowledge grows, it becomes easier and easier to get rid of the Karma of the past. Inasmuch as causes which are working out to their accomplishment, all come within the sight of the Soul which is approaching its liberation, as it looks back over past lives, as it glances down the vista of centuries along which it has been slowly climbing, it is able to see there the way in which its bonds were made, the causes which it set in motion; it is able to see how many of those causes have worked themselves out and are exhausted, how many of those causes are still working themselves out. It is able not only to look backwards but also to look forwards and see the effects these causes will produce; so that, glancing in front, the effects that will be produced are seen, and glancing behind, the causes that will bring about these effects are also visible. There is no difficulty in the supposition that just as you find in ordinary physical nature, that knowledge of certain laws enables us to predict a result, and to see the law that brings that result about, so we can transfer this idea on to a higher plane, and can imagine a condition of the developed soul, in which it is able to see the Karmic causes that it has set going behind it, and also the Karmic effects through which it has to work in the future.

With such a knowledge of causes, and a vision of their working out, it is possible to introduce fresh causes to neutralise these effects, and by utilising the law, and by relying absolutely on its unchanging and unvarying character, and by a careful calculation of the forces set going, to make the effects in the future those which we desire. That is a mere matter of calculation. Suppose vibrations of hatred have been set going in the past, we can deliberately set to work to quench these vibrations, and to prevent their working out into the present and future, by setting up against them vibrations of love. Just in the same way as we can take a wave of sound, and then a second wave, and setting the two going one slightly after the other, so that the vibrations of the denser part of the one shall correspond to the rarer part of the other, and thus out of sounds we can make silence by interference, so in the higher regions it is possible by love and hate vibrations, used by knowledge and controlled by will, to bring Karmic causes to an ending and so to reach equilibrium, which is another word for liberation. That knowledge is beyond the reach of the enormous majority. What the majority can do is this, if they choose to utilise the Science of the Soul. They may take the evidence of experts on this subject, they may take the moral precepts of the great religious Teachers of the world, and by obedience to these precepts—to which their intuition responds although they may not understand the method of their working—they may effect in the doing that which also may be effected by distinct and deliberate knowledge So devotion and obedience to a Teacher may work towards liberation as knowledge might otherwise do.

Applying these principles in every direction the student will begin to realise how man is handicapped by ignorance, and how great is the part played by knowledge in human evolution. Men drift because they do not know ; they are helpless because they are blind ; the man who would finish his course more rapidly than will the common mass of men, who would leave the slothful crowd behind " as the racer leaves the hack," he needs wisdom as well as love, knowledge as well as devotion. There is no need for him to wear out slowly the links of chains forged long ago ; he can file them swiftly through, and be rid of them as effectively as though they slowly rusted away to set him free.

THE CEASING OF KARMA.

Karma brings us ever back to rebirth, binds us to the wheel of births and deaths. Good Karma drags us back as relentlessly as bad, and the chain which

is wrought out of our virtues holds as firmly and as
closely as that forged from our vices. How then
shall the weaving of the chain be put an end to,
since man must think and feel as long as he lives,
and thoughts and feelings are ever generating
Karma? The answer to this is the great lesson of
the *Bhagavad Gîtâ*, the lesson taught to the warrior
prince. Neither to hermit nor to student was that
lesson given, but to the warrior striving for victory, the prince immersed in the duties of his
state.

Not in action but in desire, not in action but in
attachment to its fruit, lies the binding force of
action. An action is performed with desire to enjoy
its fruit, a course is adopted with desire to obtain
its results; the Soul is expectant and Nature must
reply to it, it has demanded and Nature must award.
To every cause is bound its effect, to every action
its fruit, and desire is the cord that links them
together, the thread that runs between. If this
could be burned up the connexion would cease, and
when all the bonds of the heart are broken the Soul
is free. Karma can then no longer hold it; Karma
can then no longer bind it; the wheel of cause and
effect may continue to turn, but the Soul has become
the Liberated Life.

Without attachment, constantly perform action which is
duty, for, performing action without attachment, man verily
reacheth the Supreme.*

* *Bhagavad Gîtâ*, iii. 19.

To perform this Karma-Yoga—Yoga of action—as it is called, man must perform every action merely as duty, doing all in harmony with the Law. Seeking to conform to the Law on any plane of being on which he is busied, he aims at becoming a force working with the Divine Will for evolution, and yields a perfect obedience in every phase of his activity. Thus all his actions partake of the nature of sacrifice, and are offered for the turning of the Wheel of the Law, not for any fruit that they may bring; the action is performed as duty, the fruit is joyfully given for the helping of men; he has no concern with it, it belongs to the Law, and to the Law he leaves it for distribution.

And so we read:

Whose works are all free from the moulding of desire, whose actions are burned up by the fire of wisdom, he is called a Sage by the spiritually wise.

Having abandoned all attachment to the fruit of action, always content, seeking refuge in none, although doing actions he is not doing anything.

Free from desire, his thoughts controlled by the SELF, having abandoned all attachment, performing action by the body alone, he doth not commit sin.

Content with whatsoever he receiveth, free from the pairs of opposites, without envy, balanced in success and failure, though he hath acted he is not bound;

For with attachment dead, harmonious, his thoughts established in wisdom, his works sacrifices, all his action melts away.*

* *Ibid.*, iv. 19-23.

Body and mind work out their full activities; with the body all bodily action is performed, with the mind all mental; but the SELF remains serene, untroubled, lending not of its eternal essence to forge the chains of time. Right action is never neglected, but is faithfully performed to the limit of the available powers, renunciation of attachment to the fruit not implying any sloth or carelessness in acting:

As the ignorant act from attachment to action, O Bhârata, so should the wise act without attachment, desiring the maintenance of mankind.

Let no wise man unsettle the mind of ignorant people attached to action; but acting in harmony (with Me) let him render all action attractive*.

The man who reaches this state of "inaction in action," has learned the secret of the ceasing of Karma; he destroys by knowledge the action he has generated in the past, he burns up the action of the present by devotion. Then it is that he attains the state spoken of by "John the Divine" in the Revelation, in which the man goeth no more out of the Temple. For the Soul goes out of the Temple many and many a time into the plains of life, but the time arrives when he becomes a pillar, "a pillar in the Temple of my God;" that Temple is the universe of liberated Souls, and only those who are bound to nothing for themselves can be bound to everyone in the name of the One Life.

* *Ibid.*, iii. 25, 26.

These bonds of desire then, of personal desire, nay of individual desire, must be broken. We can see how the breaking will begin ; and here comes in a mistake which many young students are apt to fall into, a mistake so natural and easy that it is constantly occurring. We do not break the " bonds of the heart " by trying to kill the heart. We do not break the bonds of desire by trying to turn ourselves into stones or pieces of metal unable to feel. The disciple becomes more sensitive, and not less so, as he nears his liberation, he becomes more tender and not more hard ; for the perfect "disciple who is as the Master " is the one who answers to every thrill in the outside universe, who is touched by and responds to everything, who feels and answers to everything, who just because he desires nothing for himself is able to give everything to all. Such a one cannot be held by Karma, he forges no bonds to bind the Soul. As the disciple becomes more and more a channel of Divine Life to the world, he asks nothing save to be a channel, with wider and wider bed along which the great Life may flow ; his only wish is that he may become a larger vessel, with less of obstacle in himself to hinder the outward pouring of the Life ; working for nothing save to be of service, that is the life of discipleship, in which the bonds that bind are broken.

But there is one bond that breaks not ever, the bond of that real unity which is no bond, for it cannot be distinguished as separate, that which unites the One to the All, the disciple to the Master, the Master to His disciple; the Divine Life which draws us ever onwards and upwards, but binds us not to the wheel of birth and death. We are drawn back to earth—first by desire for what we enjoy there, then by higher and higher desires which still have earth for their region of fulfilment—for spiritual knowledge, spiritual growth, spiritual devotion. What is it, when all is accomplished, that still binds the Masters to the world of men? Not anything that the world can offer Them. There is no knowledge on earth They have not; there is no power on earth that They wield not; there is no further experience that might enrich Their lives; there is nothing that the world can give Them that can draw Them back to birth. And yet They come, because a Divine compulsion that is from within and not from without sends Them to the earth—which otherwise They might leave for ever—to help Their brethren, to labour century after century, millennium after millennium, for the joy and service that make Their love and peace ineffable, with nothing that the earth can give Them, save the joy of seeing other Souls growing into Their likeness, beginning to share with them the conscious life of God.

COLLECTIVE KARMA.

The gathering together of Souls into groups, forming families, castes, nations, races, introduces a new element of perplexity into Karmic results, and it is here that room is found for what are called " accidents," as well as for the adjustments continually being made by the Lords of Karma. It appears that while nothing can befall a man that is not " in his Karma " as an individual, advantage may be taken of, say, a national or a seismic catastrophe to enable him to work off a piece of bad Karma which would not normally have fallen into the life-span through which he is passing ; it appears—I can only speak hereon speculatively, not having definite knowledge on this point—as though sudden death could not strike off a man's body unless he owed such a death to the Law, no matter into what whirl of catastrophic disaster he may be hurled ; he would be what is called " miraculously preserved " amid the death and ruin that swept away his neighbours, and emerge unharmed from tempest or fiery outbreak. But if he owed a life, and were drawn by his national or family Karma within the area of such a disturbance, then, although such sudden death had not been woven into his Linga Sharîra for that special life, no active interference might be made for his preservation ; special care would be taken of him afterwards that he might not suffer unduly from his sudden snatching out of earth-life, but he would be allowed to pay his debt on the arising of such an opportunity, brought within his reach by the wider sweep of the Law, by the collective Karma that involves him.

Similarly, benefits may accrue to him by this

indirect action of the Law, as when he belongs to a nation that is enjoying the fruit of some good national Karma ; and he may thus receive some debt owed to him by Nature, the payment of which would not have fallen within his present lot had only his individual Karma been concerned.

A man's birth in a particular nation is influenced by certain general principles of evolution as well as by his immediate characteristics. The Soul in its slow development has not only to pass through the seven Root Races of a globe (I deal with the normal evolution of humanity), but also through the sub-races. This necessity imposes certain conditions, to which the individual Karma must adapt itself, and a nation belonging to the sub-race through which the Soul has to pass will offer the area within which the more special conditions needed must be found. Where long series of incarnations have been followed it has been found that some individuals progress from sub-race to sub-race very regularly, whereas others are more erratic, taking repeated incarnations perhaps in one sub-race. Within the limits of the sub-race, the individual characteristics of the man will draw him towards one nation or another, and we may notice dominant national characteristics re-emerging on the stage of history *en bloc* after the normal interval of fifteen hundred years ; thus crowds of Romans reincarnate as Englishmen, the enterprising, colonising, conquering, imperial instincts re-appearing as national attributes. A man in whom such national characteristics were strongly marked, and whose time for rebirth had come, would be drafted into the English nation by his Karma, and would then share the national destiny for good or for evil, so far as that destiny affected the fate of an individual.

The family tie is naturally of a more personal character than is the national, and those who weave bonds of close affection in one life tend to be drawn together again as members of the same family. Sometimes these ties recur very persistently life after life, and the destinies of two individuals are very intimately interwoven in successive incarnations. Sometimes, in consequence of the different lengths of the Devachans necessitated by differences of intellectual and spiritual activity during the earth-lives spent together—members of a family may be scattered and may not meet again until after several incarnations. Speaking generally, the more close the tie in the higher regions of life, the greater the likelihood of rebirth in a family group. Here again the Karma of the individual is affected by the inter-linked Karmas of his family, and he may enjoy or suffer through these in a way not inherent in his own life-Karma, and so receive or pay Karmic debts, out-of-date, as we may say. So far as the personality is concerned, this seems to bring with it a certain balancing up or compensation in Kama-Loka and Devachan, in order that complete justice may be done even to the fleeting personality.

The working out in detail of collective Karma would carry us far beyond the limits of such an elementary work as the present and far beyond the knowledge of the writer; only these fragmentary hints can at present be offered to the student. For precise understanding, a long study of individual cases would be necessary, traced through many thousands of years. Speculation on these matters is idle; it is patient observation that is needed.

There is, however, one other aspect of collective Karma on which some word may fitly be said : the relation between men's thoughts and deeds and the aspects of external nature. On this obscure subject Mme. Blavatsky has the following :

Following Plato, Aristotle explained that the term στοιχεῖα [elements] was understood only as meaning the incorporeal principles placed at each of the four great divisions of our cosmical world, to supervise them. Thus, no more than Christians do Pagans *adore* and *worship* the Elements and the (imaginary) cardinal points, but the " Gods " that respectively rule over them. For the Church, there are two kinds of Sidereal Beings, Angels and Devils. For the Kabalist and Occultist there is one class, and neither Occultist nor Kabalist makes any difference between the " Rectors of Light " and the " Rectores Tenebrarum," or Cosmocratores, whom the Roman Church imagines and discovers in the " Rectors of Light," as soon as any one of them is called by another name than the one she addresses him by. It is not the Rector, or Mahârâjah, who punishes or rewards, with or without "God's" permission or order, but man himself—his deeds, or Karma, attracting individually and collectively (as in the case of whole nations sometimes) every kind of evil and calamity. We produce *Causes*, and these awaken the corresponding powers in the Sidereal World, which are magnetically and irresistibly attracted to—and react upon—those who produce such causes; whether such persons are practically the evil-doers, or simply "thinkers" who brood mischief. For thought is matter, we are taught by Modern Science; and "every particle of the existing matter must be a register of all that has happened," as Messrs. Jevons and Babbage in their *Principles of Science* tell the profane. Modern Science is. every day drawn more into the maëlstrom of Occultism;. unconsciously, no doubt still very sensibly.

" Thought is matter": not of course, however, in the sense of the German Materialist Moleschott, who assures us that " thought is the movement of matter "—a statement of almost unparalleled absurdity. Mental states and bodily states are utterly contrasted as such. But that does not affect the position that every thought, in addition to its physical accompaniment (brain-change), exhibits an objective—though to us supersensuously objective—aspect on the astral plane.*

It seems that when men generate a large number of malignant Thought-forms of a destructive character, and when these congregate in huge masses on. the Astral Plane, their energy may be, and is, precipitated on the physical plane, stirring up wars, revolutions, and social disturbances and upheavals. of every kind, falling as collective Karma on their progenitors and effecting widespread ruin. Thus. then collectively also Man is the master of his destiny, and his world is moulded by his creative action.

Epidemics of crime and disease, cycles of accidents, have a similar explanation. Thought-Forms

*The Secret Doctrine, i. 148, 149.

of anger aid in the perpetration of a murder; these Elementals are nourished by the crime, and the results of the crime—the hatred and the revengeful thoughts of those who loved the victim, the fierce resentment of the criminal, his baffled fury when violently sent out of the world—still further reinforce their host with many malignant forms; these again from the astral plane impel an evil man to fresh crime, and again the circle of new impulses is trodden, and we have an epidemic of violent deeds. Diseases spread, and the thoughts of fear which follow their progress act directly as strengtheners of the power of the disease; magnetic disturbances are set up and propagated, and re-act on the magnetic spheres of people within the affected area. In every direction, in endless fashions, do men's evil thoughts play havoc, as he who should have been a divine co-builder in the Universe uses his creative power to destroy.

CONCLUSION.

Such is an outline of the great Law of Karma and of its workings, by a knowledge of which a man may accelerate his evolution, by the utilisation of which a man may free himself from bondage, and become long ere his race has trodden its course, one of the Helpers and Saviours of the World. A deep and steady conviction of the truth of this Law gives to life an immovable serenity and a perfect fearlessness : nothing can touch us that we have not wrought, nothing can

injure us that we have not merited. And as everything that we have sown must ripen into harvest in
due season, and must be reaped, it is idle to lament
over the reaping when it is painful; it may as well
be done now as at any future time, since it cannot
be evaded, and, once done, it cannot return to
trouble us again. Painful Karma may therefore well be faced with a joyful heart, as a thing to
be gladly worked through and done with; it is
better to have it behind us than before us, and every
debt paid leaves us with less to pay. Would that
the world knew and could feel the strength that
comes from this resting on the Law. Unfortunately
to most in the Western world it is a mere chimæra,
and even among Theosophists belief in Karma is
more an intellectual assent than a living and fruitful
conviction in the light of which the life is lived.
The strength of' a belief, says Professor Bain, is
measured by its influence on conduct, and belief in
Karma ought to make the life pure, strong, serene
and glad. Only our own deeds can hinder us; only
our own will can fetter us. Once let men recognise
this truth, and the hour of their liberation has
struck. Nature cannot enslave the Soul that by
Wisdom has gained Power, and uses both in
Love.

THE THEOSOPHICAL SOCIETY.

THE Theosophical Society is an international body which was founded at New York, on the 17th of November, 1875. Its objects are :

FIRST —*To form the nucleus of a universal brotherhood of humanity without distinction of race, creed, sex, caste or colour.*

SECOND.—*To promote the study of Aryan and other Eastern literatures, religions, philosophies and sciences, and demonstrate the importance of that study.*

THIRD. —*To investigate unexplained laws of nature and the psychic powers latent in man.*

Of these three objects the first is the only one which is

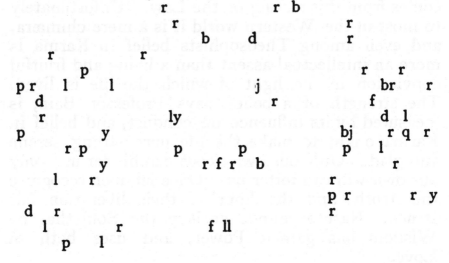

The members of the Society are connected by an ethical rather than by an intellectual bond, and their unity rests on etc.—will be forwarded on application to the General Secretary.

FEES AND DUES.

All applications for membership must be accompanied by (a) an entrance fee of five shillings, English (or the equivalent), and (b) the current annual subscription, which for English-reading members is five shillings (or the equivalent), and for all other members 2/6 (or the equivalent).

Fees and dues may be remitted in special cases.

All cheques, postal orders, etc., to be made payable to the General Secretary, G. R. S. Mead.

GENERAL OFFICES AND OFFICERS.

President, Col. H. S. Olcott, Adyar, Madras, India; Vice-President, A. P. Sinnett, 27, Leinster Gardens, London, W.

EUROPEAN SECTION.—General Secretary, G. R. S. Mead, B.A. (*Cantab*), 19, Avenue Road, London, N.W.

AMERICAN SECTION.—General Secretary, Alexander Fullerton, 42, Irving Place, New York, U.S.A.

INDIAN SECTION.—General Secretary, Bertram Keightley, M.A. (*Cantab*), Theosophical Society, Benares, India.

AUSTRALASIAN SECTION.—General Secretary, J. C. Staples, 42, Margaret Street, Sydney, New South Wales, Australia.

SCANDINAVIAN SECTION.—General Secretary, Dr. Gustaf Zander, Medico-Mekaniska Institutet, Jaktvarfsgatan, 4, Stockholm. Sweden.

OFFICERS OF EUROPEAN SECTION.

GENERAL SECRETARY.—G. R. S. Mead, B.A. (*Cantab*).
TREASURER.—Hon. O. S. F. Cuffe.
ASSISTANT-SECRETARY.—C. W. Leadbeater.

AUDITORS.—A. J. Faulding and M. U. Moore, M.A.
EXECUTIVE COMMITTEE.—Mr. A. P. Sinnett and Dr. W.
Wynn Westcott (Great Britain); Mons. Arthur Arnould
(France); Señor José Xifré (Spain); Mynheer W. B. Fricke
(Holland); the Treasurer and General Secretary.
EUROPEAN HEADQUARTERS.—19, Avenue Road, Regent's
Park, London, N.W.

BOOKS.

Introductory.

	s.	d.
The Key to Theosophy. H. P. Blavatsky	6	0
Esoteric Buddhism. A. P. Sinnett	3	6
Re-incarnation. Dr. J. A. Anderson ...		6
The Seven Principles of Man. Annie Besant		0
Re-incarnation. Annie Besant		0
Death—and After? Annie Besant		0
Karma. Annie Besant ...		0
The Astral Plane. C. W. Leadbeater ...		0
The Birth and Evolution of the Soul. Annie Besant		0
What is Theosophy? Walter R. Old		0

For More Advanced Students.

Isis Unveiled. H. P. Blavatsky	42	0
The Secret Doctrine. H. P. Blavatsky ...	45	0
The Theosophical Glossary. H. P. Blavatsky	12	6
A Modern Panarion. H. P. Blavatsky	15	0
Five Years of Theosophy. ...	10	0
The Self and its Sheaths. Annie Besant ...	1	6
The Building of the Cosmos. Annie Besant	2	0

Ethical.

The Voice of the Silence. Trans. by H. P. Blavatsky	2	6
The Bhagavad Gîtâ. Trans. by Annie Besant, 4s., 2s.	0	6

F

In the Outer Court. Annie Besant	2	0
Light on the Path. M. C.	1	6
The Light of Asia. Sir Edwin Arnold	3	6

Pamphlets.

H. P. B.: In Memory of Helen Petrovna Blavatsky, by
   some of her pupils.   ...   1 0

Theosophy and its Evidences. Annie Besant   3

Why I became a Theosophist. Annie Besant   4

In Defence of Theosophy. Annie Besant ...   2

The Sphinx of Theosophy. Annie Besant   3

The Meaning and Use of Pain. Annie Besant   3

Devotion and its Place in the Spiritual Life. Annie
   Besant 0 2

Vegetarianism in the Light of Theosophy. Annie Besant

Theosophy in Questions and Answers. Annie Besant

Theosophy and Christianity. Annie Besant

Theosophy and its Teachings. Annie Besant

The Masters as Facts and Ideals. Annie Besant

The Place of Peace. Annie Besant   ...

An Introduction to Theosophy. Annie Besant

A Rough Outline of Theosophy. Annie Besant

Theosophy and Occultism. G. R. S. Mead

Yoga : The Science of the Soul. G. R. S. Mead

Theosophy and Religion. G. R. S. Mead. For distribution 2s. 6d. per 100.

Short Glossary of Theosophical Terms. Annie Besant
   and Herbert Burrows   ...   ...

Studies in the Secret Doctrine. I. Cooper-Oakley and
   A. M. Glass   0 4

   The Theosophist. Edited by Colonel H. S. Olcott, P.T.S.
£1 per annum, post free.

   Lucifer, monthly, founded by H. P. Blavatsky, and edited
by Annie Besant and G. R. S. Mead ; 17/6 per annum, post
free.

Mercury, edited by J. T. Walters, Palace Hotel, San Francisco, Cal., U.S.A. ; one dollar per annum.

All the above can be obtained at the Offices of the Theosophical Publishing Society, 7, Duke Street, Adelphi, W.C., where also full catalogues of books can be obtained.

THE REFERENCE LIBRARY.

There is a Reference Library at Headquarters, open to Members of the Society only, containing the majority of works of reference found in Theosophical literature. The Library is open from 2 to 10 p.m.

THE LENDING LIBRARY.

There is a Lending Library at Headquarters, open to the public. The subscription is 10s. for 12 months, 6s. for 6 months, and 1s. 6d. for 1 month. Postage to be paid by the subscriber.

Those desiring further information can obtain it by applying in person or in writing to the General Secretary of the European Section or to any of the Officers of the various Lodges in the United Kingdom and Europe.

G. R. S. MEAD,
Gen. Sec. European Section.
19, Avenue Road, Regent's Park, London, N.W.

All orders for periodicals and books should be addressed to the Manager, Theosophical Publishing Society, 7, Duke Street, Adelphi, London, W.C., and NOT *to the General Secretary.*

LONDON:

PRINTED BY THE WOMEN'S PRINTING SOCIETY, LIMITED,
66, WHITCOMB STREET, W.C.

Lightning Source UK Ltd.
Milton Keynes UK
UKOW05f0210210417

299596UK00003B/74/P